HEY EV~~~~~~
TEENS LOVE
MIRACLES

Ruth Reid

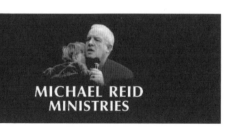

Michael Reid Publishing
49 Coxtie Green Road
Brentwood Essex CM14 5PS
England

First edition 2006
Reprinted, Second edition 2008

Printed in England

ISBN 1-871367-33-6

All scripture quotations are taken from the King James Version of the Bible unless otherwise indicated.

ACKNOWLEDGEMENTS
To all those in the production department who have helped me, with great patience, to get the manuscript for this book together.

DEDICATION
To the Church of Tomorrow - our children of today.

Contents

Bishop Michael & Rev Ruth Reid

Introduction

I f you are anything like me, I always read the introduction to a book because there you often catch a glimpse of the author that shows what makes them really tick. It is more than a snapshot, it is a personal glimpse into the being of the writer that you usually do not get in the rest of the book. I love people and that makes me want to read the rest of the book because I feel I have had a personal introduction to them. The next few paragraphs will help you to know me and what makes me tick. Hopefully it will intrigue you enough to read the rest of the book as I am convinced that we have something valuable to contribute to the body of Christ everywhere.

What prompted me to write this book?

I am writing this book to share my passion for the children and teenagers of tomorrow's church with other pastors, youth workers, teachers and parents. Most pastors are parents, many parents and pastors are teachers, so your roles are interchangeable. If at times the content seems a bit too theological for parents or too practical and personal for pastors - remember the range of readers I am trying to reach. You are the main influences on a young person's life and as such are vitally important. **The main theme of this book is the vital cooperation necessary between the home, church and school in reaching and keeping the young people for the Church of tomorrow.**

I have been so stirred in my being for many years to make life in Christ as relevant, challenging and exciting for today's generation of young people, as it has been for me. My own encounter with Christ was so real that it changed everything for me as his encounter did for my husband, Bishop Michael Reid, founder of Peniel Church and Michael Reid Ministries. I have not lost the wonder and amazement of how God has led us over the years and been so faithful to provide in every way. We have found that when we are passionately concerned about some issue, God will always provide the answers. He probably put the concern there in the first place! **God is always a problem solver not a problem creator - nothing is too hard for Him.**

Burning questions resonated in my heart first and foremost concerning my own children, but it soon became much more inclusive of all the young people in the church that we started together. How was I going to co-operate with God, instead of being a hindrance, so that my children would not be turned off Christianity as they grew older? Was there any way that I could prevent Christianity from being as boring and irrelevant as it had seemed to me as a young person? What was the answer for each generation to know their God and make a real difference in that generation? I knew that God must have the solutions because He cares for and loves tomorrow's Church so much more than I do.

What were my sources?

When considering a topic for my thesis for the Doctor of Ministry degree from Oral Roberts University in Tulsa, Oklahoma in the United States, I knew that I would have to write on a subject about which I was passionately concerned. It would have been hard to keep the momentum going throughout the process of writing a thesis without being motivated by very strong inclinations. Some horrifying statistics came to my notice about the loss of children and young people from the church in the UK that pierced me through to the heart. I began to realise that God wanted me to share the solutions that He has shown my husband and me over the many years of pastoring one church where children and young people are in abundance and very few are lost to the world. I have called these principles the 'Peniel Model' and for my thesis attempted to measure which ones had the most influence on the young people.

This book will explain to the reader how we came across the principles that God taught us. We were not aware at the time that they could possibly have any wider application other than for the   youth immediately in our care. However, as we realised the desperate loss of young people to the Church in England and other parts of the world, we have come to the understanding that of course God knew the situation and prepared us for such a time as this. Are you the reader asking any of the same questions as I did? Is there an urgency within your spirit that something must be done to keep young people in the church? Does your heart ache when you see the children of Christians depart from the faith when to all intents and purposes it looks as though the parents have done everything to bring them up in 'the fear and admonition of the Lord?' If this is so, then this book is for you!

The last generation of teenagers in the church?

1

Is this the Last Generation of Teenagers in the Church?

t is a favourite pastime of the media to try and shock with statistics about one disturbing trend in society after another. In order not to be constantly worried by these statistics, we turn off to their message and we become inured to their content. However there are a few statistics that are very relevant that you need to know in order for you to have any grasp of the urgency of the situation and how desperate it is for the church to **WAKE UP.** The former Archbishop of Canterbury, George Carey, said that **the church was one generation away from extinction** at a Church of England Board of Mission in 1999.[1] Was he being too dramatic and just trying to shock? Surely he was only talking about the Anglican Church?

The complete figures for the loss of young people from the churches in England during the 1990's show that the rate amongst the under 15s was a thousand a week - 52,000 a year. The greatest overall loss was amongst teenagers aged 10-19 years.[2] It does not take great logic to wonder where the Church of tomorrow is going to come from and what sort of church it is going to look like. Are the statistics better elsewhere in the world? Yes, but the trend there is also downwards. Take the United States for example. George Barna, the American Christian Polster, states that there may be a drop of as much as 50% in church attendance by teenagers, once they can make their own choices or have moved away from home.[3]

The teen years are so vital

The majority of people who become Christians are born again or converted during their teenage years. I recently heard the figure of 60% quoted by David Cerullo, CEO of the Christian TV channel, Inspiration, at the launch of their international network in the House of Commons in London (May 2005). Bill Wilson, founder of Metro Ministries, an outreach centre for inner city children based in New York, writes that they consider that if a young person is not reached for Christ by the age of fourteen it is almost too late. There are too many other powerful influences at work that deter older teenagers. I quote from his book, *Whose Child is This?*, "If we are going to see a transformation in the coming generation, we've got to instil values while the children are young. We concentrate on what we do best - and believe that when those we train become parents, they will make a real difference. When a young person reaches age fourteen or older, it is almost too late - the die is cast. I believe in preventative medicine. It is a lot easier to make boys and girls than to repair men and women."[4] It is clear that the teenage years are vital everywhere, whether they come from New York or a little village in England.

One last statistic
(for this chapter at least!)

This is the statistic that pierced me through to the heart and has constantly stirred in me ever since I heard it, even more so than the others quoted earlier in the chapter. **Only 1 in 6 children of Christian parents in England will be in church by the age of 25 years.** It took days before I recovered from the shock of hearing this quoted by Peter Brierley of Christian Research UK in an interview in 2004. The understanding of the ramifications of this statistic are so far reaching that it is almost incomprehensible. Did I lose hope at the enormity of the task? At first it almost overwhelmed me. But God is in control!! Since then it has become an exciting challenge to see what the God of the Impossible will do to reverse   'the extinction of the church in the next generation.' The principles behind the success of keeping young people in the church of the 'Peniel Model' will be a part (however large or small) of God's solution. Otherwise He would never have laid them upon mine and my husband's heart.

What are these principles? Find out in the next chapters.

Peniel Academy opens in 1982

2

Where Did We Start?

I started with the realisation that **Jesus Christ is building His church**. His church does not go into extinction, nor does it fail. He has an answer for every generation. The teenagers of today are as much God's concern as every generation has been throughout history. I will demonstrate from a few examples from the Bible how God has been faithful in every generation. What has looked like a hopeless situation, God has always turned around and used people to do it. God has made a way for us to build strong, stable marriages and families, so that the children can grow up in a secure environment. Does this mean that God is not interested in helping where things have broken down and the ideal is lost in a mess of broken relationships? Of course not, but He will straighten the situation out and restore things if we will let Him. **God is in the restoration business.**

Nothing is too hard for God

Abraham and Sarah tried to go ahead of God and make their own arrangements to provide a child. The promised baby was so long in coming that they gave up hope and forgot to trust God's promises. They no doubt regretted it afterwards. Ishmael proved a liability thereafter, and they certainly had some thorny family issues with Hagar. However, God still spoke again to Abraham and Sarah through the two heavenly visitors who told them the good news that Isaac would be born. As Abraham accompanied them on their journey, they turned toward Sodom, when God spoke to him yet again. These heavenly visitors carefully explained to him God's reasons for including Abraham in His plans for Sodom and Gomorrah. God could trust Abraham with this knowledge because He knew that Abraham would be faithful to teach his family the right way to live and follow God, unlike his nephew, Lot (Gen. 18:19). God's trust in Abraham never turned out to be misplaced with regard to teaching his family to follow the Lord. That is why the story of Genesis continues with the next generation - that of Isaac.

Think about the Children of Israel in bondage to Pharoah and the next generation in danger of extinction because of the edict to kill all the male children. God had the solution ready. The feisty Hebrew midwives pretended that the Hebrew women were so strong and healthy, compared to the Egyptian women, that the women had their babies too quickly and they could never get to the birth on time. As a consequence they were never able to obey the edict to kill the boys as soon as they were born. The first chapter of Exodus records that **the opposite happened to that which Pharoah intended - that generation increased mightily in numbers!**

God chose Moses as the deliverer for the children of Israel. He had already been saved from death miraculously by the ingenuity of his mother (Ex. 2:2-10). However, despite being brought up in Pharoah's palace, he landed up in the backside of the desert looking after his father-in-law's sheep because he killed an Egyptian who was torturing a Hebrew slave. God knew that Moses needed encouragement so He introduced Himself to him as the God of his father and of Abraham, Isaac and Jacob at the burning bush in the desert (Ex. 3:6). God was reminding Moses of his heritage and how faithful He had been in the lives of his forefathers. If He was good to them, He would find a solution for the terrible predicament of His people. Moses was the solution to save that generation.

God's faithfulness never ends

Maybe you are thinking - but what about that same generation that perished in the wilderness because of their unbelief? True, but God saved Joshua and Caleb from that generation to lead the next generation into victory in the Promised Land. Rahab's testimony to the spies forty years later showed that the enemies in the Promised Land were already   defeated   in   their hearts for all that time (Josh. 2:11). God is so good, He always gives us the victory!

At the end of his life, Joshua gathered all the tribes and their leaders together to speak very seriously to them, and challenge them about whether the next generation would continue to follow the Lord (Josh. 24). He gave a brief account of their history thus far and how God had intervened on their behalf on many occasions. Joshua marked the occasion by leaving a memorial of a great stone under an oak tree in order to try and refresh their memories as to what had happened on that day when they had promised Joshua that they would all serve the Lord. His words had good effect for one generation, but after that things began to go downhill until the

Bible records "every man did that which was right in his own eyes" (Judg. 17:6). Keeping the Children of Israel focused on God was a constant problem throughout the generations, as recorded in the Old Testament. **God laid down clear guidelines for every family to follow in order for each generation to know their God.**

What about the New Testament?

Are there any examples of God's faithfulness to each generation? Paul testifies to God's faithfulness to Timothy's family. God was the God of Lois, Eunice and Timothy (2 Tim. 1:5). Paul reminded Timothy of his heritage of 'unfeigned faith' from the example of his mother and grandmother. He encouraged him not to fear but to take hold of everything that God had given him to pursue the task set before him even though he, Paul, was in prison. Paul also testified that he could thoroughly recommend Timothy to the Philippian church as someone who would "naturally care for your state" and that he would be more faithful than all the others with whom he worked (Phil. 2:19-20). Timothy also served Paul in the work of the gospel as a son to a father.

The promise is to you and your children

God's promises are yea and amen for today. He is always faithful to keep His word to us. On the Day of Pentecost, in Acts 2, Peter explained that the new covenant was even better than the old, drawing from the prophetic passages of the Old Testament that foretold of that day. **The outpouring of the Holy Spirit was for them and their children.** A well known man of God from the 19th century, Charles H. Spurgeon, reiterated in one of his sermons that

God had always intended that children and young people would be able to receive the promise of the Holy Spirit as in Acts 2:39. Firstly, Spurgeon refers to the geographical nature of the promise, "But the passage, instead of speaking of anything being a privilege to certain people and their children, expressly declares that, while it is their privilege, and their children's privilege, it is equally the privilege of all that are afar off, 'as many as the Lord our God shall call.' That is to say, that the great covenant promise, 'Whosoever shall call on the name of the Lord shall be saved,' is meant for you, is meant for Hottentots, is meant for Hindoos, is meant for Greenlanders, is meant for everybody to whom the Lord's call is addressed."[5]

Spurgeon then goes on to expand the promise to the future generations to whom the promise would apply, not just geographically, "Addressing all the Jews who were gathered around him, Peter said, 'The promise is to you.' Looking forward to all the future generations of Jews that were to be born, he added, 'and to your children'…. Comprehending the vast population of the whole globe, throughout all time, Peter says, 'This promise is to you all,' "Whosoever shall call on the name of the Lord shall be saved."[6]

Parents, pastors and teachers alike should take great encouragement from these promises. It has always been God's intention that the children of believers would come into the same experience of the Holy Spirit as their parents. It is so important for people who deal with children and young people to operate from a basis of true faith; not having a sentimental humanism towards them that excuses sin, but faith in the God who keeps His promises. **He is the God of each generation.**

How does it work in practice?

Where did I get the ideas about the principles of God for families? The Bible is full of God's dealings with different families. In the beginning, God made man and woman to be together and to be fruitful and multiply. Marriage was instituted by God. As much as marriage was always part of God's plan from the beginning, the result of the union between man and woman in having children was also commanded as a blessing by Him from the outset. God told Adam and Eve to "Be fruitful, and multiply, and replenish the earth, and subdue it" (Gen. 1:28). In verse 31 the Bible records that on the sixth day God was pleased with His creation of male and female, plus all His other creation. He was delighted to bless everything He had made with the capacity to reproduce its own kind. Gordon Wenham, the Bible commentator, points out, in Genesis 1, that verse 31 (NIV), "And God saw all that he had made that it was really very good," is constructed in such a way as to emphasise "the perfection of the final work."[7]

God believes in marriage - He instituted it!

Prophetically Jeremiah spoke of the restoration of the relationship between God and His people. One of the blessings of restoration for them would be that the voice of joy and gladness of the bride and bridegroom would be heard in the cities of Judah and Jerusalem (Jer. 33:11). **The literal meaning demonstrates the desire of God for happy and strong marriages** - how much more in the new covenant with better promises would this be the case. This promise is not just for Judah and Jerusalem it is for everyone who is a child of God. In this day and age people fear the commitment of marriage, so they are either postponing marriage until much later than before or they are not getting married at all. Thus children are born much later in a marriage and there are fewer of them. Christians do not have to fear in the same way; they can be confident of God's blessing upon marriage and having children.

The blessing of having children runs as a very common thread throughout these accounts. 'Plenty of children' was listed among the special blessings reserved for those who love God, to a thousand generations, in chapter 7 of Deuteronomy: "And he will love thee, and bless thee, and multiply thee: and he will also bless the fruit of thy womb..." Once again this is an old covenant blessing: how much more is this true for those of us who are living in the reality of the new covenant.

Again in Jeremiah 32, God promises that He will gather His people again from where they have been scattered. He says that He will give them "one heart, and one way, that they may fear me for ever, for the good of them, **and their children after them.**" God is not going to miss out the children from the blessings that He promises the parents. Does it sound very reminiscent of the Day of Pentecost when they were all gathered together in one place and were of one accord (Acts 2:1)?

God is not in the business of failure

For our generation and beyond, my husband and I understood that God would not be involved in building a failing church. In the late 1970's, when we looked around at what was happening in the UK, there seemed to be only a few bright sparks of churches where God was moving in miracle power amongst the general mass of dead religion. We realised that, if necessary, the church that we were building together with God, and all the people who contributed, would be like an oasis in the desert. We did not get much encouragement from other pastors. In fact, it was just the opposite! However, the opposition helped us focus on what God wanted and be determined to follow His instructions. We were only too glad to follow God's directions, as He made it abundantly plain that He wanted my husband to think outside the normal parameters of 'church' and build something different. God spoke to my husband as he started the church and explained that his various encounters with different churches had given him plenty of experience of what he did not want in a church. **Now he was to build what he did want.**

Church is people - families are made up of people. Bishop Reid often says that the church is a big family and the family a small church. In those early years of building the church, we found that one of the fundamental answers was to build strong families. My husband and I found that we had to go 'back to basics' in teaching the families that were coming to the church. Even if some of the families had had previous church exposure, their family lives ranged from mildly to chronically dysfunctional. My husband taught a women's Bible study once a week on a range of different topics, but mostly to do with family life. I encouraged the women to put into practice what they were hearing.

Man's methods do not work

I had been trained as a Child Care Officer in the early 1970s, and worked near Liverpool in the north of England. My remit had been to visit and counsel dysfunctional families whose children had come to the notice of the authorities in some way or another. I became very discouraged with the attempts that I was making to help these families through various crises. I found that everything would blow apart again when, not if, the next crisis happened. By contrast, it was a revelation to me to find that the results of teaching biblical principles to this group of women at church were so different. I was delighted to see the teaching working in the lives of the families; everyone was changing for the better - the wives, the husbands and the children.

We knew that what we taught could not just be words. We had a burning desire that we should first and foremost fulfill the prerequisites for church eldership that Paul prescribed for Timothy and Titus (1 Tim. 3:4-5; Tit. 1:6). **We knew we had to be an example to the flock of God in bringing up our own children according to God's principles.** These biblical principles of child-rearing became a practical reality for us, as we raised our own three children by adhering to them, throughout the formative years of the church. We found they worked for us as well as the other families! Were we perfect as parents? I am sure we could have done better in some instances - but we are talking about God's principles for family life - they are immutable.

So I have established in this chapter that God is building His church and makes Himself known to every generation. Expect Him to be what He says He will be. **God is the wise master builder and all we have to do is follow His blueprint.** God loves His church so much more than we do. A vibrant church is upheld by strong families being built into the fabric of the building by the faithful preaching and teaching of the Word. I do not have to tell you that family and marriage have been under attack for a few decades now. Divorce rates are increasing and many families are torn apart as a result. However, I have no doubt that God has the answers for tomorrow's church and for this generation of children and teenagers. In the next chapter I will go into more detail as to how God expects the family to be structured in order to make it strong and healthy and to bring up the children in the way that they should go.

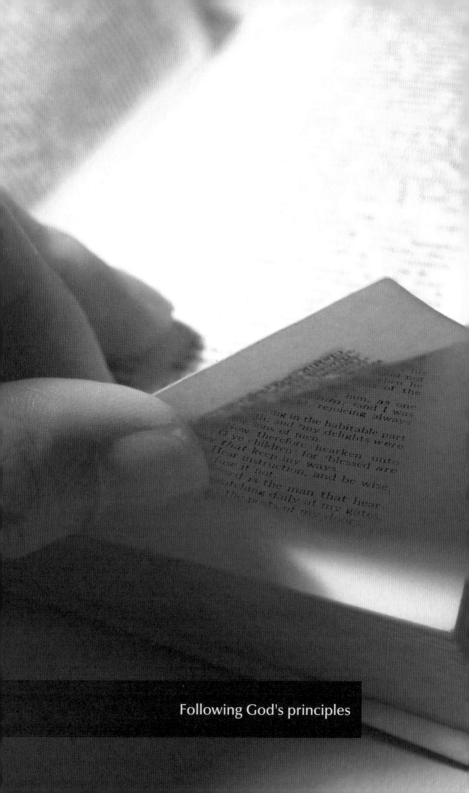

Following God's principles

3

Where Does God Start?

God does not vary with the whims and fancies of the 'experts' in family living. In the 1970's, when we were bringing up our young children, Dr Spock, famous paediatrician and health expert of the 1940's, and others, recommended allowing children complete freedom to express themselves. Guess who ended up ruling the family? The tirading two year olds who grew into troublesome teens! It certainly has not improved in the 21st century. Fads come and go in childrearing and education which have proved harmful to whole generations of children until the prevailing wisdom of the day realises that they have gone too far in the wrong direction. My husband and I discovered that **following God's principles of family living really does work and has done for hundreds of years.**

Has not our understanding of how children develop changed? Are we not more enlightened? In the UK the government is really struggling to know what to do with what they call the 'yob culture.' Friends from the US asked what was meant by the term 'yob.' When we described the youth who are out of control, drinking alcohol heavily and into drugs, they agreed that their country had the same problem. Unfortunately it is fairly universal. What is God's answer?

Fathers rule, OK

God has not changed His mind about the authority structure in a family just because 'current wisdom' denies the validity of it. In both the Old and New Testament, He made it clear that the father is the head of the household and is responsible to raise his children in the way God expects. Modern teaching, both in and out of the church, has changed the balance of authority, bowing to the political correctness of the day. I am a thoroughly happy, educated and liberated woman who recognises that God knows what is best for men, women and the family. I am very grateful that the main responsibility for the family belongs to my husband. Not that I am trying to shirk responsibility. I was the one who carried out much of the day to day caring for the children as well as being a busy pastor's wife. How wonderful it was to have a peaceful home where the children knew the boundaries and were secure and happy. It was a delight to have children and now to be blessed with grandchildren. Grandchildren are God's best invention - we can enjoy them without the daily responsibility of bringing them up!

Fathers must learn obedience to God first

God, through Moses, first and most importantly exhorted the fathers that they must love God with everything within them and internalise His commandments in their hearts (Deut. 4-6). Christensen, a Bible commentator, explains the ideas behind these verses. He writes that "Obedience is not to be a matter of formal legalism, but rather a response out of deep understanding. By reflecting on God's words (6:1), and by knowing the path of life set forth through the commandments, the people would discover for themselves the way in which God's love for them was shown."[8] Obeying God's commandments was not just a chore; they realised that God was much smarter than they were and He knew what He was talking about.

Lead by example

Once the ways of God were part of the lives of the fathers, then God turned his attention to the children. He instructed the fathers as to the importance of their duties to pass on the knowledge of all they had learnt to their children. No child will be able to accept the teaching of the parent if the parent is not the embodiment of what they are teaching - God is pointing out that the parents must live it - by example! Every opportunity to teach their children must be taken at any given moment during the day or night (Deut. 6:7). Christensen explains, "Having understood these commandments in depth, they were then responsible *to teach them diligently to [their] children (v7; cf. 4:9)*. The commandments were to be the focus of constant discussion inside and outside the home. In short they were to permeate every sphere of human life."[9]

I love the way that the next two verses of this chapter in Deuteronomy emphasise so descriptively the importance of living the commandments in reality. Moses writes about binding them on their hands, having them in front of their eyes all the time, and writing them on the doorposts of their houses. Later in that chapter Moses enlarges the concept of teaching children. (He could have read the books on modern teaching methods) When a child starts asking questions about their religious practices, every spontaneous opportunity must be taken to testify to them of the wonderful deliverance of God and all the accompanying signs and wonders (Deut. 6:20-25). **God does not want any parent, particularly the fathers, to miss any opportunity to turn the subject of the conversation onto the goodness of God and his faithfulness.**

Is what Moses taught all too legalistic? Surely we have something better in the New Covenant? Of course we do, because the life of Christ within writes all these principles in our hearts, so that the results are not by our religious efforts but by the power of God working in us. Paul says that they are for our examples (1 Cor. 10:11).

Personal glimpses!

Guess what! I made big mistakes in my first attempt at child rearing. In my training as a Child Care Officer, I had imbibed a good dose of the psychological and sociological wisdom of the day concerning families. My first child was an adorable little girl who began to rule the roost by the time she was walking. Why? I was letting her express herself and tried not to restrain her so that she would develop her personality without hindrance from me. **It was I who ended up in tears, not the baby!**

Thank God for a sensible husband who intervened before I had torn my hair out! His family had certainly not brought him up with Christian principles - so how did he know so much? He did what he has always done throughout his life; **he took the word of God at face value, believed that it would work, and implemented it.** He dealt with our little angel very firmly and showed me the way to have peace in the home. It worked! He only ever had to raise his voice slightly and look at the children before they would change their mind about continuing to do what they were doing. He is right when he claims that he very rarely had to smack any of them, but it was there as an ultimate deterrent for both of us.

Mothers rule too, OK

It goes without saying that a mother has an equally vital yet different role to play in the lives of her children. Proverbs 31 explains how the children of a 'virtuous woman' will be ever grateful for and blessed by her industry and example in the home. I was inspired by the life of Susannah Wesley who had 21 children, but took their education very seriously in their early years. Despite having so many children she determined to have a period of fifteen minutes alone once every two weeks with each child. Her two sons, John and Charles Wesley, played major roles in the Great Awakening of the 18th century.

On reading this I determined that I would spend the same amount of time every evening we were at home with each of my children, since I only had three! I would read from the Bible, or stories of miracles, or any interesting biographies of missionaries and other men and women of God, so that they were their heroes. We would also sing and pray together. I stopped when they reached their early teenage years, because they were old enough to enjoy reading by themselves. My husband encouraged them to continue to keep their faith alive through the same inspiration drawn from saints of old and any current ministry who was making a mark in the world. They would ask him for recommendations for good books to read from his very well stocked library!

Dr James Dobson, the Christian guru of American child rearing, explains in his book, *Parenting isn't for Cowards*, that mothers in particular suffer from a great burden of guilt when things do not go well with their child rearing efforts. Guilt paralyses people from acting with confidence when faced with the tremendous challenges that each stage of a child's life can bring. If the parents back off from their God given responsibilities, then the child rules by manipulation of one parent against the other. When this happens the atmosphere at home is fraught.

The loss of parental authority

Parents feel disenfranchised by the attitude of governments and schools as the family is undermined by legislation and hostility towards parents 'interfering' if they question what is happening to their child. In the UK there are moves by the government to ban smacking as a form of punishment that parents are allowed to enforce with their children. In many European nations, any form of corporal punishment is banned. However, traditionally, the church through the ages backed parents and encouraged them to take full responsibility for their children in discipline as well as in education throughout their lives. Many of the major denominations took schooling very seriously and invested a great deal in their educational programmes setting up schools and universities throughout the previous centuries.

Parents are the most natural evangelists to their children

It is a good idea to learn from Charles H. Spurgeon, who pastored a church of many thousands called the Metropolitan Tabernacle at the Elephant and Castle in London. He preached a sermon on Deuteronomy 6:23 called *Brought Out, To Be Brought In,* explaining that **parents are the most natural evangelists to testify to their children of the wonderful works of God.** He pleads with parents to take every opportunity, "Perhaps, my friend, there is no greater testimony that you can bear, which will be so useful, so interesting, and so striking, as the testimony of what you have yourself seen and handled of the Word of life. Tell the gospel as you find it in the Bible, but set it in the frame of your own experience of its preciousness. Tell your son how you sinned, and how the Lord had mercy upon you; tell him how he met with you, and how you were brought to seek his face, how you were born again, how you received a new heart and a right spirit."[10] Spurgeon's two sons grew up to serve God in the ministry.

If you love your children, then you will train them

Parents do affect the behaviour of their children, especially when they do not love them enough to discipline and train them. The record of Eli's sons' behaviour in comparison to Samuel is most poignant. It is the boy Samuel who is told by God all that will happen to Eli and his sons (1 Sam. 3:1-19). Samuel has to tell Eli the bad news of their horrible end! Once again, I will turn to another of Spurgeon's sermons where he brings out the irony of the situation for Eli and applies a lesson for all parents to take heed as to how they bring up their children. "As often as he looked upon the gracious child, Samuel, he must have felt the heartache. When he remembered his own neglected and unchastened sons, and how they had made themselves vile before all Israel, Samuel was the living witness of what grace can work where children are trained up in God's fear, and Hophni and Phineas were sad specimens of what parental indulgence will produce in the children of the best men."[11] These accounts are in the Bible for us to take heed of the lessons contained in them, even though we are living in the New Covenant.

To train or not to train - that is the question!

Theologians have different ways of interpreting a key verse that is so important in the upbringing of children. Of course, the verse that I am referring to is Proverbs 22:6! "Train up a child in the way that he should go: and when he is old, he will not depart from it." Some would say that this verse means that parents should make sure that the child is encouraged according to his gifts and abilities. Others interpret this verse to mean that even if your child leaves Christianity once they are no longer under your influence, when they are advanced in years they will return to the fold. I am glad to say that my husband and I took this verse as a promise from God, that He would be faithful to keep our children if we were faithful in bringing them up according to God's principles.

We have not been disappointed!!

There is another controversial verse in Proverbs that has, and always will, keep the debate going. This verse has to do with the means of disciplining a child. Governments in the 'western world' have increased the controversy by making it illegal to follow this advice. Proverbs 13:24 says that a father who will not discipline his children with the rod hates them, conversely, those who do discipline their children when it is necessary; love their children. The biblical commentator, Allan Ross, explains the principle clearly, "Too much lenience and too much harsh discipline are equally problematic. The balance comes while the child has room to grow while learning the limits."[12] God is not a monster who would recommend harsh treatment. Hebrews 12:5-8 explains God's heart in the matter of discipline. He is our heavenly Father and I am grateful that He cares enough to get so closely involved in my life. I have the security of knowing that I cannot go wrong without knowing it. Paul pleads for fathers not to be too harsh in their discipline of their children so that they provoke them to anger, but to bring them up "in the nurture and admonition of the Lord" (Eph. 6:4).

The need for consistency

The discipline and training of children takes time, effort, determination, patience and consistency. In fact, without God's help, it is an almost impossible task. It is so easy to let things slide and allow the children to get away with things. It is easier to let the boundaries slip gradually, than make the effort to present them with an alternative way of behaving and keep them occupied with wholesome things. Dr Martyn Lloyd Jones, a famous preacher from the last century, explains, "There is nothing more annoying to a child than the kind of parent whose moods and actions you can never predict, who is changeable, whose condition is always uncertain. There is no worse type of parent than he who one day, in a kindly mood, is indulgent and allows the child to do almost anything it likes, but who the next day flares up in a rage when the child does scarcely anything at all."[13] Thus he sums up the need for consistency most aptly.

Is anger ever right?

One of the problems in Christian circles is the teaching on anger: where suppression is the only answer. Wrath ("fits of rage," NIV) is clearly listed by Paul as one of the works of the flesh. **Anger is a God given gift that used in the right way, provokes us to action.** Hence, Paul writes about the subject to the Ephesian church, "Be ye angry, and sin not; let not the sun go down on your wrath; neither give place to the devil" (Eph. 4:26-27). Paul's warning not to give place to the devil implies that unrestrained anger will give the enemy advantage to attack. Forgiving and forgetting must come as well so that the child knows complete restoration. Lloyd-Jones sums up the meaning of these verses, "Anger is something that is placed in us by God; it is a capacity within man which results in his being roused by the sight of certain things. And the result is that it is a priceless and precious thing."[14] The gospels record occasions when Jesus got angry when he saw what was happening in the temple, and it certainly provoked him to action!

My point is that unless we allow the wrong actions

and attitudes of our children to provoke us to action, we will let things slide. This does not mean that we are on their case for every little thing, but that there are secure boundaries drawn. Paul warns fathers not to provoke their children to anger (Eph. 6:4). Children are happy when they know what the boundaries are, and the amount of friction and moaning is drastically reduced. Life at home becomes a pleasure. There is a reality programme on the TV in the UK where an experienced nanny shows parents what they are doing with their children to make life hell at home. Most of the advice she gives is to do with setting boundaries and sticking to them. It has become very popular and the nanny has made plenty of money!

God's principles concerning raising children are not rocket science, but Dr Dobson and others reject those who proclaim them as smug and complacent, because they have never had to deal with difficult children. Dr Dobson draws from the example of Esau and Jacob who were different from their mother's womb,[15] but he does not allow for the transforming power of the Holy Spirit. Once again the teen years are the most vital for them to be introduced to a Jesus who loves them and is alive and real and still does miracles today.

I have found that children who have been taught obedience in the first three years of their lives rarely exhibit the 'normal' levels of rebellion in their youth. Children are different and some will be more difficult than others to train in obedience. Every person needs to be taught to control their own spirit, Proverbs is very clear on this matter. It is much better for a person to rule their own spirit than to take a city (Prov. 16:32). To highlight the distinction, I have recently had similar reactions from two non-Christian fathers when I enquired about their teenage children. Before they had time to think about what they were saying they expressed horror at the problems that they were encountering - tantrums, rudeness, sulky silence, and that they could not say anything without it being interpreted as wrong. I felt so sorry for them, realising again that many parents endure teenage years feeling absolutely helpless to do anything about the situation. Dare I say it, we enjoyed our children's teenage years. Of course we had our times of worry and anxiety over them; but the overriding confidence we had lay in our complete dependence upon God who would be faithful to keep them, if we followed His principles.

You need to live in the real world!

Other ministries and people who have had unfortunate experiences of family life, such as divorce and remarriage or children lost to the world, do sometimes level this criticism at us. The real world means Christian Parents do sometimes lose their children to the world.Of course this does happen - it would be ridiculous to deny it! But exceptions never nullify the word of God. Jesus was a perfect son to His Father and obeyed Him in every way and yet He recognized this problem with his stories of the prodigal son and the lost sheep in Luke 15. I asked my husband, Bishop Reid, one day what was the difference between the two stories and it prompted him to preach on the subject.

The prodigal son lived in his father's house so he was able to enjoy all the benefits of being born again into the family of God - translated into our terms of reference. We all know the story - he decides to leave home and asks for his portion of the inheritance and goes off and does his own thing, ending up in a mess. Finally, he comes to his senses and decides to go back home. Bishop Reid pointed out that the Father did not spend all his time searching for his son - he let him go to find out the consequences of his actions. He was delighted when he returned and had been looking out for him but he never interfered with the process of him 'coming to himself.' If your child had a real experience of God and yet somehow still left all that he knew - relax and let God and circumstances work in his or her life to bring them back home. God is faithful!

What is different about the lost sheep? The lost sheep was also in Father's house - it wandered off by itself from the sheep fold and was completely lost. Bishop Reid likened this to children of parents who have never known God or become a Christian, especially if the parents became Christians after they left home. They really are lost in which case the parents need to really seek them and find them in order for them to have an opportunity of hearing the gospel that they have never had while they were at home. If and when they respond to the good news and become Christians, then they bring them home rejoicing!!

We are well aware that churchgoers of today face the problem of divorce far more frequently than in previous generations. As Peniel Church expands, the families that join are often unchurched, so it is more likely that they will bring serious amounts of 'baggage' with them. We believe firmly in marriage as a lifelong commitment - this is clearly a biblical principle, and we are not going to apologise for it. However, Bishop Reid will always support the right of a woman or a man to be free of a physically or mentally abusive situation if that is what they really want and all other avenues have been exhausted. Regrettably, divorce is sometimes the only answer.

Our experience with broken and/or blended families and step-children is that the vast majority of situations improve tremendously as the parents, or parent, have a life-changing encounter with God. Then they have the confidence to adjust their family lifestyle according to the principles of God. Their children usually respond very favourably to consistent boundaries drawn, and to the positive peer pressure that they have from others in the church and school. God's promises remain the same and He is always faithful. The past is over and each one has a new beginning in God. Even the most serious baggage can be left behind at the cross, never to be remembered any more (2 Cor. 5:17&18).

Of course the most important thing that can happen to a child or teenager is that they are born again. This is the work of God alone, but parents and the church can make a difference by providing every means for this experience to take place and to remain intact throughout their lives. In this chapter I have drawn attention to God's principles for parents, so that there is an understanding about how a family should be structured. But, don't give up and think it is all down to the parents, saying **"The answers for teens can't just be the parents - what about peer pressure and all the influences of the world?"** You are right - there is more to it…

Children love church!

4

How Important is Church?

What comes first when choosing a place to live? The logical choice is usually governed by the proximity to the parent's place of work or the children's schools. The beauty of the location, or the house of your dreams, or the proximity to family and friends are often considered very important. Would you look for a church after all the other things that are necessary to the well being of your family are in place, or do you make finding a church with life your first priority? God intends for everyone to belong to a church and there is a place where you belong that He will provide for all who want to 'seek first the kingdom of God.' He knows more than you do that your children need to experience a living church - He is the God of each generation! **Teens need to know that God is real and that they can see Him in action in the life of the church and their daily lives.** The priority is to find out where God wants you to fit in the body of Christ, so that you and your children can be built into a habitation for God, corporately and individually.

Leslie Francis, professor of Practical Theology, and William Kay, Senior Lecturer, both at University of Wales, Bangor, did a study of teenage religion and values and found that teenagers that went to church had a different attitude to the prevailing feeling of helplessness amongst the others. They observed that, "While 38% of non-church goers think that they can make a difference to the world's problems, the comparable figure for weekly churchgoers is 58%. This suggests that the kind of faith these Christian young people espouse is not purely contemplative and academic, but practical and noticeable. To underline this point, a comparison between non-church going atheists and churchgoers shows that it is the churchgoers (58%) who feel relatively effective in the face of the world's problems and the atheists (35%) who feel relatively powerless."[16] The young people have grasped the fact that they are helped by a greater power than themselves.

What is distinctive about teens' faith?

Wesner Fallaw, a pastor and writer on education, has some insightful observations on the subject. He explains that as adolescents grow in faith, they develop a very decisive view of life - there are no shades of grey. "After the age of twelve years he is no longer interested in how things work; he wants to know why. He begins to generalise. Abstractions as well as particulars have now come within his province...Parents, friends, standards, values, issues of daily life are re-examined - often with incisiveness and a tendency to discard some things and accept others with pronounced zeal."[17] **Young people are rarely taken in by hypocrisy and they will often have very definite views about most things.**

According to Fallaw, the adolescent must feel free to develop more and more his independence and yet know that he has a place in the church. "What home and church need to achieve through their united efforts is the sort of guidance which enables an adolescent to know he is understood, that his independence is guaranteed as rapidly as he demonstrates readiness to function independently and that the adult world of parents and church has a place for him."[18] It is imperative that young people feel that they are valued for their talents and skills and given opportunity to express them. Thus they feel a valued part of the church community. For example, the TV and media department of Michael Reid Ministries would not run without the help of the young people. They love to be involved in these areas. To be in the forefront of technological development of computers and media outlets as methods of reaching the lost is the kind of challenge they relish.

Mark Cannister, an associate professor of Christian Education at Gordon College, Wenham, Massachusetts, points out that the teenage years are very important because teens are going through many changes and are open to ideas of spirituality. He stresses that, "These are critical years in which the evangelical church has a unique opportunity. **At no other time in a person's life are so many options considered, changes made, and lives shaped. Youthful minds and open hearts have numerous questions that require honest responses as they try to establish an identity that might include Christ.**"[19] (I have added the bold emphasis) It is a great time of opportunity to influence young people for the rest of their lives. If they make the right choices at this stage in life, they will be set up for the future.

What are we looking for?

So, are we looking for a kind of 'spiritual hot house' environment where teens will make the right choices about their futures? No way! **Decisions that teens make as a result of being mentally persuaded for Christ will not last.** There has to be a real encounter with God that changes everything. They must be convinced without a doubt that "they know that they know that they know" that God has met them, and Christ lives within. Such a relationship with God will be all they need for the rest of their lives, as long as they are part of a living church, nourished "by that which every joint supplies" in the body of Christ. The Apostle Peter recommends that a new born baby should 'desire the sincere milk of the word' (1 Pet. 2:2). They need to hear and respond to the preaching of the Word in the power of the Spirit so that they grow up healthy.

Teens love reality

As a teenager I was bored with church - I went to please my parents because my father was an Anglican vicar. It would have been a bad example for me to stop going to church. Thank God, I attended a Youth Camp before I went to university where I encountered a different type of Christianity that made me realise that there was something more to it than I thought. It started me on a journey that took seven years before I finally understood that I could not automatically call myself a Christian because my parents did. I needed a radical nature change and the only way that could happen was by a life changing encounter with God. God revealed himself to me in a remarkable way when I was 25 years old.   It is so important that parents do everything within their power to attend a church where their teens will be introduced to the reality of Christianity. **Teens want to see what works - miracles and transformed lives with no sham or hypocrisy.**

One of the greatest assets of the teen years is that this is the time of life when they carry the least baggage and are up for any challenges that life throws at them. Barna points out, "Of all the different age-defined populations, high school and college students feel most capable of taking audacious risks in virtually every dimension of their lives. They rarely feel encumbered by the tyranny of personal history and remain unconscious of societal limitations."[20] "What about the damaged teens? It is not the same for them," I can hear you say. Why do you think they get involved with the wrong side of life? They are looking for the same challenges as the 'normal' teen but it is misdirected.

My husband joined the Metropolitan Police in London looking for excitement and challenge in his early twenties. He could not bear the thought of being 'chained to a desk' in local government as a surveyor. I wanted to go to China as a missionary and be the second Gladys Aylward, but God wanted me to be the first Mrs Reid! I was very happy with the exchange and our lives have never lacked excitement or challenge. On God's instruction we built a spiritual home, the church, for our family and all the other families who have joined us since the beginning.

Hey Everyone! Teens Love Miracles

The title of this book is "Hey Everyone! Teens Love

Miracles." I chose this title after conducting a survey amongst the teenagers in Peniel Church for my thesis, in order to find out what part of the services they liked most! **Without fail their answer was they enjoyed watching the miracles the best.** They witness healings and miracles happening nearly every Sunday in church. So many of the families in the church have come and stayed because God intervened in a miraculous way in their own lives. Bishop Reid has some favourite sayings which emphasise the priority that he puts on miracles as an essential part of the ministry of a church. "No miracles? No Jesus! Wherever Jesus is there are always miracles. If you don't go to a church where you find deaf ears unstopped, the lame walking and the blind seeing you haven't found a church yet." **If the preaching does not sow the seed of the word of God of the good news about miracles (the miracle of new birth included), then there will be no harvest of miracles!**

What intrigued me more was to find that the next favourite part of the service was the preaching! It was nearly up there with the miracles! You can see for yourselves on the graph below. I have always found my husband's preaching stimulating and interesting but I was not expecting the teenagers to have a similar reaction. **Jesus' instructions to the disciples were to preach, teach and heal when He sent them out. Teenagers agree totally with His emphasis (Matt. 9:35)!** What a shame that so many churches feel they need to provide other things to attract teens - rock, rap (and whatever is the latest craze in contemporary music), clubs and special services. Parents and most grown ups are excluded too.

In a survey that I did amongst Pastors and others that I

invited for a two day seminar for my thesis, I found them to be in agreement with the current 'wisdom' in providing entertainment for teens in order to attract them to church. However, many of them changed their opinion after the seminar when they were shown the results of my survey amongst the teenagers in our church. They also had an opportunity to observe and communicate with the young people of the church when they visited Peniel Academy, our church school for church members' children only. You can see from the graph below that they began to realise that Jesus' method of preach, teach, heal has not lost its power and does not need to be replaced with contemporary and new ideas. **What is missing is the 'demonstration of the Spirit and of power' (1 Cor. 2:4) of an apostolic ministry that Paul writes of to the Corinthian church.**

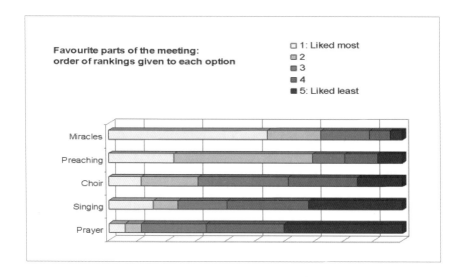

The graphs below show the comparison between the answers of the pastors and others who attended the seminar lectures I gave concerning how to retain young people in the church.

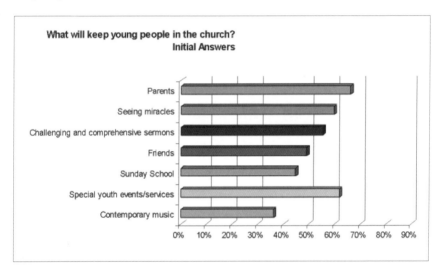

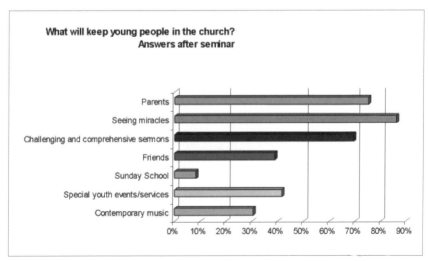

When asked to choose the main attributes that described Peniel Church, the young people selected 'helpful' as the most descriptive (see graph opposite). 'Challenging' and 'faith building' followed very closely. The next two choices of adjectives were 'exciting' and 'stimulating'. The largest variation between boys and girls was on 'challenging' and 'exciting', with the boys choosing those descriptions slightly less frequently. Overall there was very little disagreement. Before you think that these answers are too good to be true, I would point out that the questionnaires given for the children to fill in were

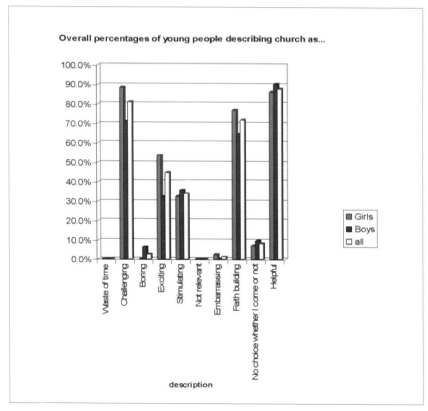

completely anonymous. They were not pressured to conform or please in their answers.

The difference explained

Approximately thirty percent of Peniel Church consists of children under 18 years. This shows that it is a flourishing family church with plenty of young people. Peter Brierley of Christian Research UK was invited to do a research report on our church in November 2001. He remarked in his conclusions on "The mature believing young people." He then went on to elaborate more, **"The children and young people who attend Peniel are markedly different from the majority of such in other English churches, and would suggest that the policy of integration of the services and throughout the church is not only important for the church but important for their faith and wellbeing."**[21] An outside observer remarking on the difference in the young people!

What was that you just read above in bold? The children go to all the church services! Do you mean to say that they even sit through the preaching? Peter Brierley believes that this is important for their faith and wellbeing. That certainly is different. It will probably shock you to discover that the children are introduced to the complete services at the age of two and have to learn not to distract everyone else from being able to concentrate on what is happening. What a blessing for the parents when they discover that if their children can do it in church, they can also do it at home if well occupied! If the children attend Peniel Academy they are expected to make notes on the sermon from the age of six or seven, and they are marked by the teacher in school.

Sunday morning attendance at church is compulsory.

Why have we done this? Bishop Reid is adamant that children and teenagers should not think that church is a separate activity from which they are excluded. **He wants church attendance to be a shared family experience.** Barna remarks, "Teenagers rarely embrace Christianity if their family has treated faith as a Sunday-morning experience; it must be the focal point of their lives."[22] The sermons should be interesting and easy enough for children to understand. Spurgeon is reputed to have remarked that preachers must be understood by five year olds otherwise they are preaching over people's heads.

The importance of good role models in the ministry

The encouragement and challenge of the teaching on family life at Peniel Church has prompted the parents' declaration that they had been given a good role model for their own lives. This has in turn influenced their family's lives. It is so important for the ministry of a church to be able to plead like Paul. "Be ye followers of me, even as I also am of Christ." (1 Cor. 11:1). William Yount, professor of Education at Southwestern Baptist Theological Seminary, expressed this concept succinctly when he wrote, "The church is a body of Believers drawn from all walks of life and placed together in a social context because of their faith in Jesus Christ. The church is a context for social learning, in which those who are mature spiritually become the models for converts and young Christians. The Bible provides the content for learning; the life and work of the church provide the social laboratory where principles are converted into lifestyle."[23] It is so important that parents are a model for their family and that they in turn are challenged and encouraged by the ministry in the church.

Barna expresses the importance of ministry to teenagers thus: "Teenagers matter. Your ministry to teenagers - whether you are a senior pastor, a youth pastor, a youth worker, a teacher or parent - matters. You are shaping the future of the nation. You are determining the future of the Church. You are affecting the character and souls of the emerging leaders of the world. **What a challenge! What a privilege! If you like to be where the action is, and want to make a difference in the world, there may be no more strategic ministry for you to accept than to work with teenagers.**"[24] (I have added the bold emphasis). It is part of the prophetic ministry of the church to prepare for the future in this very practical fashion. Jesus Christ is building His church (Matt. 16:18), so what better activity to be involved in than to prepare young people in every way to be equipped to take their place in the Church of tomorrow.

Bishop Reid and I do not do not push young people into ministry; it is God who calls and commissions. If it becomes clear that they are called of God then we would do everything to enable them to fulfill what God wants them to do. Each one is encouraged to use their talents in every way possible to further the kingdom of God in whatever field of employment they choose. It is reminiscent of the way in which God spoke to Oral Roberts, Chancellor of Oral Roberts University, and told him that his students needed to go out into every man's world and be a light there.[25] As we travel in the US we find that former students of Oral Roberts University are everywhere, in all walks of life, and many of them are very successful in the work place, contributing to the kingdom of God.

What about Sunday school?

In England, Sunday School and special youth activities that have been used to reach young people and keep them in the church have failed to do the job that they did so admirably in times past. Churches have had to think again and try to come up with different strategies to reach and keep teenagers interested and focused on church and a relationship with Jesus Christ.

Bill Wilson in New York has developed sidewalk 'Sunday' schools and their main Sunday school is on a Saturday. Once again, a tremendous amount of energy, time and effort is put into the children. Metro Ministries have deliberately sought to find different ways than the norm to attract the children. Every child who attends Sunday school is visited at home once a week by one of the Metro team. Bishop Reid has preached in the churches in Brooklyn and the Bronx that have grown up as a result of 25 years of work in those areas. He loves to do it. We have ridden on the bus with Bill Wilson to collect the children. It was wonderful to see the children pouring out of their homes responding to the klaxon and the police siren that tells them that the bus is coming.

Michael Reid Ministries will not be developing the same strategy because God has led my husband and me very differently. Whatever way something is done to rescue this generation of children from being lost to the church, we are thrilled. **They are the future of the church!**

Peniel Academy 2007

5

The Peniel Model

For the purposes of my doctoral thesis at Oral Roberts University, I called the way that we have developed at Peniel Church over the years in keeping our young people 'The Peniel Model'. I am not entirely comfortable with this concept because my husband and I are wary of the 'how to' of methods. I certainly do not expect you to try and adopt everything you have read about in this book into your situation. Every church and ministry is unique! However there are principles that you will be able to draw from and find useful. The Peniel Model starts and ends with the most important factor that has made everything possible - God: to Him be all the praise and honour for what He has done! We have depended completely on His direction and guidance. Jesus Christ is building His church. God spoke to Bishop Reid the same words that He spoke to Moses, "See, saith he, that thou make all things according to the pattern showed to thee in the mount" (Heb. 8:5).

Peniel Church has stood the test of time for thirty years under the leadership and guidance of the man called by God to build it. It has grown steadily and now it is often difficult to find seats for all who come from far and wide, as well as the regular congregation. You will have already realised that the church and ministry are unusual in many respects. Bishop Reid did not follow man's pattern for church. He was not afraid to be different, and do things differently, although he never did things just to be different. The church comes first in everything within Michael Reid Ministries; although there are other arms of the ministry such as the school (Peniel Academy), the College of Higher Education affiliated to Oral Roberts University and the University of Wales, the Global Gospel Fellowship for ministers, the television ministry, the choir and the publishing. **God is the master architect and it is only wisdom to follow His instructions for building His church.**

Preaching is paramount

Above all, Bishop Reid places a paramount emphasis on the word of God preached in the power of the Spirit, being confirmed by miracles and signs in the church. The emphasis on preaching has become unpopular in the church of the 21st century, but Bishop Reid's heroes are people such as George Whitefield, Charles H. Spurgeon, Martyn Lloyd-Jones, Demos Shakarian, Archbishop Benson Idahosa, Chancellor Oral Roberts and TL Osborn. The last four he has known personally, three of whom are or were great preachers, and they all have or had miracles attend their ministries.

It is unusual to have the combination of the emphasis on the word and miracles together. It makes for a very strong church where the people know what they believe, and are challenged to live what they hear in their daily lives. They are also privileged to see practical demonstrations of God at work in so many lives, saving and healing them.

Daryl Eldridge, a Christian educationalist, writes, "The revelation of God achieves its consummation in Jesus Christ. While Jesus was often a healer and performer of miracles, he was also a teacher. In fact, over forty eight times in the Gospels Jesus is referred to as a teacher."[26] The young people see the ministry of Jesus mirrored in the life of the church. They, unlike so many of their contemporaries, can be in no doubt that the Bible is relevant for today.

Francis and Kay found in their research in Britain that many young people wanted to get married in church and have their children baptised or christened as babies in church. However, they also state that "young people in large numbers think the church and the Bible are irrelevant and that daily religious assemblies [in schools] should not be held. Many young people think that church is boring."[27] Church is definitely not 'cool' in their estimation.

The Peniel Model, however, is vitally concerned with introducing young people to Jesus Christ, so that His life becomes a reality in them through new birth. It helps them to keep this faith alive and well into adulthood, so that they are ready to form the bedrock of the Church of tomorrow. Jesus Christ is the only one who can "keep them from falling, and present them faultless before the presence of his glory with exceeding joy" (Jude 24). Can the Peniel Model guarantee that a young person will be born again? The answer to that question, of course, is 'No'. Jesus said that a person is born again not by the will of man, but by the will of God (Jn. 1:13).

Church as a family

Bishop Reid has always insisted that church is for the whole family and there should be no separation for age, gender or culture for the main services. The people who attend the church originate from many different countries. There is a good healthy mix of all age groups, different cultures and races, men (half of the congregation) and women from all walks of life. The many visitors remark on the very welcoming and friendly atmosphere of the church and they never leave the service the same. It is an experience!

The services are lively and often follow a different pattern. The children see and experience personally miracles of healing on a regular basis, which they love. In the survey of Peniel Church, from the questions asked of the eleven to fourteen year olds, Peter Brierley deduced, "Here is a group of young children, already reasonably mature in their faith, their life and witness, who enjoy their church and its leaders, its teaching and worship, and have many friends there - and wish other friends to share the experience. There are very few churches in England with a group of such contented and understanding children!"[28] Have we tried to make the children fit a certain mould or pattern so that they turn out like this? Of course not! It is because we recognise that they are all individuals with different talents given by God, and that they are comfortable being themselves. This is the hallmark of maturity that Peter Brierley observed.

A radical departure from the norm in most churches has been that Sunday school for the children is not provided as an alternative to attending church. This has been a deliberate choice of Bishop Reid. He has seen all too often that the teachers allocated to Sunday school do not really care for the children. They alternate every week or two so that the children do not form meaningful relationships with the teachers. He believes that it gives children and teenagers the message that church is not for them but only for the adults. When the time comes for a young teenager to make the transition to attend church they are often put off by the fact that they think that it is boring or not for them. Please do not be offended if you have been a good Sunday school teacher - read on and remain open to different ideas.

I love what Luther had to say on the subject - you are never in any doubt as to what he meant! On hearing a minister complain that some of the congregation felt that it was beneath them to listen to the children's catechism read out, Luther replied, "Cursed be every preacher who aims at lofty topics in the church, looking for his own glory and selfishly desiring to please one individual or another. When I preach here I adapt myself to the circumstances of the common people. I don't look to the doctors and masters, of whom scarcely forty are present, but at the hundred or the thousand young people and children. It's to them I preach, to them I devote myself, for they, too, need to understand. Therefore, my dear Bernard, take pains to be simple and direct; don't consider those who claim to be learned but be a preacher to unschooled youth and sucklings."[29] Luther had a true pastor's heart and cared for the youth of his day.

What else do we do for the teenagers?

The church school, Peniel Academy, constitutes a

tremendous investment of time, energy, money and skills on the part of many in the church for the young people. I have devoted a complete chapter to this subject later in the book.

Here I am describing what else we do for them outside of church services.

At the end of each academic year the school organises a camp in the school grounds. The children from eight to eighteen years attend the camp. The older pupils look after the younger children and are completely responsible for them in their tents. Some of the school's former students attend the camp and organise the logistics of running a smooth operation. The children do fun activities during the day, but a time is always set aside for them to be challenged and encouraged to expect a radical encounter with God that will change their lives forever. Several meetings are arranged during the rest of the year for children in the 13 to 18 year old group, called 'Tomorrow's Church', to keep things active with the young people and to build upon what was started at the camp. Bishop Reid also takes the School Assembly for the older children on a regular basis during the term.

For the next age group (18-25 years old), who are at university or have jobs, regular meetings are held by Bishop Reid to give them an opportunity to discuss relevant issues and ask questions. This group has a week's camp in the summer held at the wonderful facilities of Brizes Park, the school premises. They are not expected to sleep in tents. They sleep in the school buildings and use all the facilities. The group is divided into different teams and each has a particular project to complete during the camp. They have a daily talk and question time with myself or Bishop Reid, or with a visiting speaker, straight after breakfast. They work during the day, and then have fun together in the evenings. This is one of the opportunities for them to express their gratitude practically for all the investment put into their lives. It is a time of fellowship together, when skills are newly learned or refined, relationships formed and the young people are challenged as to the direction of their lives. They are given every opportunity to start and/or progress in their Christian walk.

As the report from Christian Research noted, the young people are involved in all areas of the church and contribute time voluntarily in many departments. They particularly love to be involved with the television ministry, updating and expanding the web pages, singing in the choir and playing in the band, although they can only join the latter two when they have left school. They have worked so hard in their spare time to put on musical productions like 'Beauty and the Beast' and 'A Christmas Carol' at Christmas time. These involved nearly all the young people and turned out to be a tremendous success. It is amazing what hidden talent comes out in the young people when they act and it is usually the quieter ones who surprise us the most!!

"Well", you say, "What is so different from the things that we have done for our young people?" I am sure that many have tried the same or similar things, so what is it that makes it work so that you do retain the teens for the Church of tomorrow? What I have covered in these last two chapters is not the whole story. I have emphasised two very important aspects: the home and the church.

However, my husband and I have found that **no matter how much we try, what a child learns in church can easily be overridden by the influence of the home if it is pulling against the ways of God.** "Surely," you say, "if they have had an experience of God they will be able to stand with or without their parents?" Of course there are many instances where a young person has stood firm in their Christian faith despite their family. However, the church and home working together can make a tremendous difference to the young person as they explore the wider world and all the influences good and bad to which they are exposed.

There is a third factor in this equation that I want to explore with you in the next chapter. **We call it the three-fold cord - What is it?**

Brizes Park, God's provision for the school (p. 75)

The three-fold cord leads to fulfilled youngsters

6

What is the Three-fold Cord?

The idea of the three-fold cord comes from Solomon in Ecclesiastes. He declares that "If one should prevail against him, two shall withstand him; and a three fold cord is not quickly broken." When reflecting on what we had done for the young people and why they remained in the church, God made it clear to Bishop Reid that what he had instituted as the main component of the Peniel Model was indeed a three-fold cord. I have written about the first two most important strands of the cord in the previous chapters. They are the home and the church. The third strand is the school. **When all three strands, the home, church and school, pull together they form a very strong cord that provides a wonderful foundation for the child as they develop through their teenage years.**

School - the third strand of the cord

Teens spend a great deal of their time at school. So obviously school is a very important and influential part of a child's life until they are sixteen or eighteen years old. It has not always been so hard to find schools with real Christian values as it is today. In the 1900's churches still took very seriously the responsibility of educating children in the UK. The state had hardly any involvement in education. Throughout the world, it has been the Christian church that has initiated and funded schools and universities. Gradually, the Church has stepped back from its responsibility and allowed the governments of the various countries to take over.

The problem of peer pressure

All parents know that even if they try and uphold biblical standards in the home, these are constantly being undermined by forces they cannot control. As their child reaches their teenage years, parents become the enemy, and woe betide them if they try and stop them from doing what others are allowed to do. A Christian school does away with much of the conflict that the child faces in secular schools. It eliminates much of the peer pressure to go the wrong way and also the teachers will not undermine what the children are taught at home and church. The parents also need to be in accord with, and supportive of, what is taught in the school and church.

Part of this three-fold cord is that Peniel Academy is open to church members' children only. The only exceptions that are made occasionally are for children from missionary families whose parents are serving the Lord in another country. Thus it is much easier for all the families to maintain the same standards because they all hear the same teaching in church. Does it always work like that? No, there have been a few people who have thought they knew better or did not want to be bothered to provide consistent boundaries for their children. **The families and the members of the church really buy into the idea because they can see that it works. They cooperate together on every level to educate their children: benefit and responsibility go hand in hand.**

There is a rule that people must attend the church for at least a year before they qualify to send their children to the school. They must also be contributing financially (by tithing) and in other practical ways. We would not want people to disturb their children's education only to find that they disagreed with something and had to change the child's school yet again.

It is often wrongly assumed because of the outstanding exam results that we have a policy of selection according to intelligence, as practised by most private and grammar schools in Britain. Peniel Academy prides itself on being truly 'comprehensive.' Each child has the opportunity to develop, both academically and in the full expression of a wholesome character. However, there are no selection processes other than the ones outlined in the paragraph above. If the parents are church members according to the above criteria, then their children qualify for admission.

What makes it different?

If church, home and school cooperate consistently, we have found that there will not be the discipline problems faced by secular schools. I happened to read the headline in a local newspaper at the beginning of the a school year, September 2004, that demonstrates what problems other schools have to face. "WARNING FOR UNRULY

PUPILS - ZERO TOLERANCE CRACKDOWN ON BAD BEHAVIOUR."[30] The article went on to explain that the school in question had employed a new headmaster who was trying to lay down the ground rules with the parents and pupils before the start of the new school year. *The Times newspaper*, in an article investigating the attitudes of 18 to 30 year olds, quoted *The Times Educational Supplement* as having done research and found that "Teachers now cite poor behaviour as the biggest single obstacle to their work." The article goes on to say that other research done by the Government "shows that 62,000 pupils were permanently or temporarily excluded from school during the summer term of 2003, 17,000 of whom were disciplined for attacking teachers or fellow pupils."[31]

Critics and curious people alike ask the question all the time as to whether our children are too protected and unable to cope with life in the 'real' world. To the contrary, I found from my questionnaires for my thesis that the young people have very few problems adapting to university life or the work situation when they leave school. Vince Avery, a former student of Peniel Academy reported to our church newspaper, *Trumpet Call*, "Looking back I could not have asked for a better education. All the pupils at Peniel are encouraged to achieve to the best of their ability and to give 100% to whatever they lay their hand to do. This work ethic coupled with biblical Christian principles gives a solid foundation for when you leave school and go to University, and then on to the work place."[32] **Pupils are well grounded in their faith, know what they believe and are not disturbed by the different standards they encounter.** Employers and universities alike ask for additional young people from

Peniel Academy because they know that they will be hard working, honest and have integrity.

Where is the recipe for success?

When David Blunkett was the Minister for Education in the Blair administration, he remarked that he would like to bottle church schools' recipe for success and pass it on to all schools.[33] Faith schools are amongst the best in the UK. "While academic results are important, many parents say they choose church schools because of the values they uphold."[34] However, the number of church schools reduces considerably after the child reaches the age of eleven years in the UK. These teenage years are the most vulnerable where a young person is often influenced by so many other things. I want to show you that it is possible even to exceed the success of faith schools. (Faith schools is a generic term that includes all faiths)

What is your recipe for success?

In 2005, Peniel Academy had a full inspection because the school had applied to become members of the Independent Schools Association (ISA). The ISA is a prestigious accrediting body whose inspections are authorised by the government. The inspection lasted five days so it was very thorough. At the end of each day the leader of the inspection team would give the headmaster of the Senior School an update. **He remarked upon the mystery of the recipe for success of the children in the school that he and the other inspectors were observing each day.** He explained that the mystery lay in the fact that the school accepted very ordinary children (no selection other than church members' children). The teachers were good but not outstanding, although very hard working and caring. How could the children turn out like they did at the end of school amongst the top high fliers in the country? They go on to some of the best universities and get good degrees, some of them have won the top prizes in their subjects.

I have inserted here the first part of the summary of the report of the inspectors so that you can see for yourself what others say about the school, teachers and children. You can go to the ISA website (www.isaschools.org.uk) and read the full report.

MAIN FINDINGS

Overall Summary

1.1   The unique collaboration of teachers and parents, united by common Christian values and beliefs, produces young people who leave the school with the highest standards of academic achievement and sporting success. At the same time, these young people are confident and assured, strengthened by their faith and with a strong sense of service. Nevertheless, there is room to clarify the structure of governance and management and to evaluate more rigorously the effectiveness of the school, as a basis for determining its future direction and extending its already considerable success.

What the School Does Well

1.2   The school has many strengths, the most important of which are the following:

- Against the background of a strongly Christian ethos, pupils develop very high personal standards.
- Academic standards are very high, both in absolute terms and in relation to pupils' attainment on entry.

- The care that the school exercises for pupils' well being, and the support and guidance they receive, are exemplary.
- The commitment and devotion of all staff make a major contribution to the success of the school.
- Parents make a major contribution to the school, both in practical terms as teachers and assistants of various kinds and in the support they give to their children's learning.
- The school has achieved outstanding success in table tennis.

However, I am starting at the end before I have explained the beginning. I will show you how we arrived at such an enviable place with the children who have been through the school and church. Are you curious as to the answer to the mystery that the inspectors found? Read on...

Mystery explained

In 1982, my husband and I founded Peniel Academy. We were both very challenged by the situation that our own children faced as they approached secondary or high school age. I was prepared to teach the children at home rather than expose them to all the negative influences that they would face at school, for example, peer pressure, unsupportive teachers. However, we realised that many other parents were in the same situation, so it was best to cater for all the children in the church. We were taking on a tremendous responsibility - to educate other people's children and do a better job of educating them than they would have elsewhere. **God has been faithful and we have ended up far exceeding our wildest dreams and imaginations - is that not just like Him!**

God always provides

God provided the ideas, personnel and the finance as I will explain. Bishop Reid always tells people to start with what they have, not to tell others that they have a vision, and expect them to provide. **God is our source!** Bishop Reid of course was the main instigator and inspiration for setting up Peniel Academy, with the help of Peter Linnecar, a dear friend and member of the church. Peter Linnecar had been a teacher in the state system and was conversant with all the government regulations concerning starting an independent school. The school started with two trained teachers and some very willing helpers most of whom had graduate education and 17 primary and secondary school children. For the first few months we used a large converted garage cum stable block for the school until we were able to complete purpose built accommodation.

To show you how far the school has come in 25 years - as of September 2006 the number of children attending the school is 76 in the Primary school (5-11 years) and 68 in the senior school (11-18 years). The average class size is ten pupils. The playschool and pre-school departments have 14 children (3-5 years). There are 22 full time and 30 part time teachers, 15 teaching assistants, and 18 full and part time ancillary staff. The numbers are increasing all the time as more and more people attend the church. "Well," you think, "of course it is the small classes that make the difference." Obviously, they do help, but there are lots of other factors which I will explain below.

God-given idea

Bishop Reid had several clear philosophies concerning how he wanted the school to operate and spent a great deal of time at the beginning making sure that both teachers and parents understood how the ethos of the school would vary from the norm. His primary motivation was that he felt clearly directed by God to start a school. Peniel Academy was founded as a natural outworking of church life to prepare and develop the Church of tomorrow.

In order to make this happen we had to find a suitable property. We looked at several different properties for over a year and finally we found the property that we knew God wanted us to have. However, the owners suddenly changed their minds and told us it was not for sale. We were so disappointed! Three months later, in September 1981, God gave it to us. It had previously been occupied by a school, so that there was no planning permission to be obtained from the local government for 'change of use.' (This could have been a major obstacle!) Secondly, the money to buy the property was given very sacrificially by the members of Peniel Church. My husband and I, and Peter and Carolyn Linnecar both sold our homes and contributed the proceeds from the sales. Altogether £212,000 was collected from church members to pay for the property (£175,000). The excess was needed to renovate the dilapidated buildings and pay legal fees. What a wonderful God we serve!

Large home school

Bishop Reid did not want the school to be run on conventional lines. When trying to describe how the school functioned to a group of professors from Oral Roberts University Education Department, who were visiting in 2001, he described Peniel Academy as a big home school. Nearly all the teachers are members of the church. Many of them work on a voluntary basis, unless the person involved is the main provider for the family income. All the parents and children are members of Peniel Church. Every parent cooperates in one way or another to help the school, even if they are not teaching. There is cooking, cleaning, building maintenance, new projects, administration and classroom assistance to mention just a few of these ways. It takes much more investment of time and talents from all the parents than most other schools, but the benefit that the parents gain in knowing that they have really contributed to the success of their children is very rewarding. They have done everything to give their children the best start in life they can.

The school is not run as a business that has to make huge profits. The sacrificial giving of time and money means that the fees that are charged are a third to half of the normal cost of sending a child to a private school. This is done deliberately so that all members of the church can afford to send their children to the school.

God's continuing provision

Once God starts something, He always maintains the necessary provision. The school was expanding and bursting at the seams of the purpose built school block that had been constructed on the church site in 1984. God always blesses more than we can ask or think. He knew our predicament, and gave us a property that has never ceased to amaze us. The purchase of the buildings at Brizes Park in 1998 was entirely from donations of church members. The price was £1.3 million because there was a tremendous amount of renovation work needing to be done. The donations were so generous that the church was able to purchase the buildings completely debt free plus fund the renovations. Brizes Park is an eighteenth century country mansion set in seventy five acres of beautiful park land. It is reputed to be one of the finest country homes in the whole of East Anglia. (A large portion of south east England comprising three counties) God has been that good!!

In 2002 and 2003 a new classroom block for the infant and junior school was built at the new school premises at Brizes Park. Most of the interior work was done voluntarily by parents and members of the congregation, which considerably reduced the capital cost. Once again the project was completed debt free. As the school is able, and God provides more and more, renovation work is being completed to improve and expand the facilities for the children on an ongoing basis.

Child-centred education

From the beginning, Bishop Reid wanted the teachers to understand that they were not just to assume that the school would operate the same as the state schools where they had taught previously. Each child was to be treated as an individual and encouraged to develop to their maximum capacity. He believes that each person learns and assimilates information at his or her own pace since the capacity, capability, background and set of experiences is unique. 'Child-centred education' does not mean that the child is the prime mover in the pace and type of subject they want to study. **It means that every child is treated as an individual and the 'key' for that child's life is sought by the teachers.**

At Peniel Academy the teacher's relationship with the child is viewed as highly important. They need to find the key that inspires each child. This key could be different in every child's life - be it music, art, different sports, verbal expression, writing, reading, languages, maths or science, amongst many others. Once a child has succeeded in one area and has gained confidence in that area, that confidence will always spread to other areas and they will begin to flourish. In the Parent Prospectus for the senior pupils of Peniel Academy one of the aims of the school is listed thus: "To help each child develop to his or her full potential - mentally, physically, emotionally and spiritually, bearing in mind the varying needs and abilities of each child." The small size of the classes lends itself to the child getting much more individual attention.

Economic forces are not what drives the school. As long as the school is breaking even there is no pressure on the head teachers to increase class sizes solely in order to make a profit. The school grows naturally as the church increases in size which it has done steadily over the years. People have wondered why we have not taken the opportunity to make plenty of money by expanding the school more rapidly.

We have resisted their pressure because we wanted to remain within the parameters that God had set.

Holistic approach

Another aspect that Bishop Reid insisted upon was that the approach to education should be holistic; developing the child, body, mind and spirit. Many years later, he found out that his ideas were mirrored in Chancellor Oral Roberts' philosophy in the establishment of Oral Roberts University. Chancellor Oral Roberts quotes from a report written about the purposes of the university in 1970. "It is the purpose of Oral Roberts University, in its commitment to the historic Christian faith, to assist the student in his quest for knowledge of his relationship to God, man, and the universe. Dedicated to the realisation of Truth and the achievement of one's life capacity, the University seeks to graduate an integrated person - spiritually alive, intellectually alert, and physically disciplined."[35] It is always good to have his ideas confirmed by such a person whom Bishop Reid really admires.

Peniel Academy started sport in a small way with table tennis in order to fulfill the purpose of training the body. Table tennis was chosen because the school was small at the beginning and both boys and girls could play it individually and together. It is a non-contact sport which reduces the risk of injuries. The school now has an outstanding record in the sporting world in table tennis which has remained the main sport. The children have won innumerable awards over the years and currently are the best school in the country for table tennis. In 2008 both boys and girls under 17 teams from the school were selected to represent England and play in the World Schools Table Tennis Championship in Malta. A variety of other sports is also played. In this way the children develop fitness, stamina, perseverance and competitiveness.

It has become politically incorrect for children to be taught to be competitive in the education world, but Bishop Reid wanted to encourage children always to aim for the highest. He explained in a seminar on education recently that the body is important and if the pupils are not healthy due to bad nutrition and lack of exercise they will not learn well either. Another benefit of participating in sporting events all over the country is that the children learn to mix with other children who are not Christians. They stand up for themselves. Some parents and teachers always travel with the children as they go to other countries to represent their school or their country in table tennis.

Music and the arts are very much encouraged as well. When the school first started every child learned at least one instrument. The church orchestra today consists of many of those first pupils who have now become proficient on different instruments. Most of the children who take these subjects at GCSE and A level pass their exams with flying colours. The school prospectus explains that the children are also encouraged in the performing arts with various plays and shows that they perform during the year 'in house.' They also enter competitions for recitation and drama with great success. This is all part of developing the whole person and gives them confidence to speak in public.

Education, not indoctrination

Bishop Reid is very clear that the school is for education, not for indoctrinating the children in Christianity. As he always says, **"It is not an evangelistic arm of the church nor an indoctrination centre but a place where children will be equipped for life, both temporal and eternal."** Most of the teachers are Christians, the ethos of the school is Christian and the children follow the required national curriculum 'Religious Education' syllabus. They have school chapel and pastoral care classes once a week. However all the other subjects are taught as they would be in any school following the national curriculum. The school is not used for evangelistic purposes, that function belongs in the church. Bishop Reid is confident that the children will find all they need spiritually by attending the church. Sunday morning chapel at the church is compulsory for parents and children alike during term time.

Memorisation

At the school which Bishop Reid attended he had to learn large portions of Shakespeare word perfect and be able to repeat it out loud. He also had to write the same passages out word and punctuation perfect. He felt that it would be an excellent idea for the children to learn Bible passages instead of Shakespeare. He still remembered passages of Shakespeare: how much more would it benefit the children to be able to remember passages of scripture throughout their life. When he mooted this idea to the teachers at the start of the school, they were sure that the children would never manage such a task. However, he insisted that the teachers give the idea a good effort. A system of passages was worked out varying in length and difficulty for each age group and the children rose to the challenge beautifully. **By the time a child leaves the school they know a great deal of the New Testament by heart as well as important passages from the Old Testament.** Parents learn them as well as they are the main people to teach the passages to their children at home.

At the time that Bishop Reid insisted upon memorisation of the Bible for the children, once again, he was not consciously aware what an important part memorisation played in Hebrew education. Later, as I began to research for my thesis, I discovered that it would have been a very substantial part of the way that Jesus learned as a child. **Hebrew children in Jesus' day would have had to repeat their lessons back to the teacher verbatim.** It was because of this that Jesus was able to confound and astonish the doctors and teachers in the temple (Lk. 2:46&47). He would have known great tracts of the Scriptures which would have been brought to His remembrance with understanding.

Marvin R. Wilson, a leading scholar on Christian-Jewish relations, points out the gospels could never have been written with such accuracy if memorisation did not pay such a key role in Hebrew education. He emphasises that, "The importance of memorization can be well illustrated by the writing of the Gospels. A number of years elapsed - many scholars think two decades or more - between the death of Jesus and the writing of the first Gospel. During this time the early Church (primarily Jews at this point) kept alive and preserved many of the sayings of Jesus by means of the Jew's keenly trained memories."[36] How does memorisation fit for the modern day when teaching methods are generally against the more formalised methods of teaching? **At Peniel Academy it is believed that early and consistent memory training is a key factor in later exam success.**

Education - the key to life

Bishop Reid believes that education is the key to life and that if Christians are to be 'the head, and not the tail' (Deut. 28:13) in the society in which they live, they need to be leaders in their field of expertise. The children are taught not to be afraid of hard work and they learn the necessity of the work ethic. By example the children understand that learning is for life in that their teachers are still studying to improve their skills.

The results of the education received at Peniel Academy are exemplary. Nearly every child graduates with more than enough in the results of their A levels to gain entrance to the university of their choice. Three of the former students of Peniel Academy were awarded top prizes in their subject upon graduating from university in 2004. As a result of the inspection of the school by the Department for Education and Employment, Her Majesty's Inspector, Mr Robertson, reported that **"Pupils were highly motivated, keen to learn and delightful. Attainment exceeds what would be expected nationally in relation to the capabilities and ages of the pupils concerned."**[37]   Official public league tables for 2007 placed Peniel Academy as third in the country, based on GSCE and A Level results.[38] Many of the young people who have left university have excellent jobs and are succeeding in the vocation of their choice. Most of them have continued to attend Peniel Church; some have married and now have children attending the school.

Peniel Academy is part and parcel of the success in keeping young people in the church, but as I have pointed out, it is definitely not the whole story. It is more like the icing on the cake - there would still be a cake even if there were no icing! By the cake, I mean the church and the home. I have explained all the different principles that govern the running of the school. The school fulfils many of the needs in a young person's life, helping them with their current and future behaviour, education, resisting peer pressure, coping with persecution for their faith, a good work ethic, finding a job or university course, and success in life. To quote the Peniel Academy Parent Prospectus, "Each pupil is recognised as an individual, unique in God's eyes and each with the abilities and talents that need to be developed."

The parents, when surveyed anonymously, were very positive about what their teenagers were gaining or had gained from attending Peniel Academy, so much so, that they and their children all said that they would send their children to the school again. The foundation of Christian values and the excellent education that they received in their teenage years have been a wonderful launch pad into life for them. The parents had only to compare the moral foundation for their children's character and lifestyle with their peers who had not had the same advantages to realise that there is a real difference in their teenagers. Most of the parents had no doubt that their teenagers would continue to go to church in five to ten years time.

When the 18-40 year olds were surveyed, they demonstrated that their faith had stayed the same or increased, with a very few exceptions, after they had entered university or secular employment. The results from these questions clearly show that the young adults in the church remain, with their faith vibrant so that it spills over into every part of their life. **They are definitely developing into those who will be 'the head and not the tail' (Deut. 28:13) in society at large, and talented young adults with so much to offer the church.**

Excellence is the 'name of the game.'

In the late 1970s and early 1980s about 40 Christian schools sprang up in Britain. This was probably largely as a response to what was happening in America with the Christian Schools Movement. Unfortunately, many of these schools are no longer in existence, although it was a mercy to the children that some of them ceased to exist as the standard of these schools was below that of the state schools. Bishop Reid says that if a Christian School cannot exceed that which the government has to offer there is no point having a school. Putting the name 'Christian' to a school is no excuse for mediocrity or worse: **the name Christian should be synonymous with excellence.** Children only have one chance at education, so Christians should not ruin the children's opportunity by poor educational standards and unqualified teachers. We can not palm off our children with second best, they are valuable to God as I am sure they are to you.

What happens when they go to university?

I do not have any statistics for the UK, but in the US, 55 percent of Christian students from Christian families are denying their faith by the time they graduate from college.[39] Going to university often involves a move away from home and church, so it is sometimes difficult for the young person to find a church to connect with that is similar to the home church. The final stage of the adolescent years is associated with great change, because they face all the decisions about their future career and/or choice of subject to study at university. According to statistics, it is another 'dangerous' time for the church and is often associated with very able and intelligent young people being lost to the church.

Just from a secular point of view The Daily Telegraph published an article written by Barbara Lantin about how difficult some students find their first term away from home when they start university. "Responsibilities come thick and fast in the first few weeks of university. Students are living away from family, amid strangers in an unknown city. Money is tight, especially in the early, high-spending weeks of term. There may be worries about whether the course is right and about accommodation, especially for those unable to secure a place in university residence." The article goes on to state that the Royal College of Psychiatrists reports on the mental health of students in higher education, "as many as 60% of first year students report homesickness and they are at a greater risk of developing mental health problems."[40] The problem needs addressing by churches as many young people are falling through the net at this stage in their lives.

As Peniel Church is within a short commuting distance of London, it has been relatively easy to overcome these problems for the young people. Bishop Reid has gone against the mistaken idea that young people need to go away to university to learn to stand on their own two feet. There is a great range of higher education available in London, with London University offering some of the best education in the country at its different colleges. There is no need for the young people to move away from home and church, so the only difference of lifestyle they face is that associated with pursuing a career or going on to some form of higher education. "Surely you are overprotecting them," you might say, "and stifling their independence." No! No! No! **If it is a time when young people are lost to the church, then we need to do something about it instead of just letting them drift away from the things of God in the name of independence.**

Another provision made for the young people is Peniel College of Higher Education (PCHE). Like Chancellor Oral Roberts, Bishop Reid recognised that this was a crucial time for young people. Peniel College of Higher Education is affiliated with Oral Roberts University (ORU) so that those students who graduate from the college hold a degree from Oral Roberts University. Since 2005, the college has also been able to offer undergraduate, masters and PhD degrees in Theology through the University of Wales. The college is expanding each term with many international students as well as indigenous applicants. These degrees from Oral Roberts University and the University of Wales offer an international accreditation that is valid the world over. Students who graduate with the ORU degree can 'walk' at the ORU campus in Tulsa, Oklahoma as well as at the PCHE graduation ceremony.

In 2005, Peniel College began a year's course designed for students who wanted to have a 'gap year' before starting their degree course at the university of their choice. This course is not all academic and provides the student with some time to earn some money. They attend some of the theology lectures that will give them a good basis for understanding the Bible and have practical training in the areas of the ministry that most suit their talents and abilities. Parents are sometimes relieved to be able to give their children another year to mature before they go on to university.

Bishop Reid says that it is so important for education to be lifelong. **Once we stop learning, we die.** We have tried to provide an opportunity for both old and young to be able to fulfill God's purposes in their lives. Acquiring skills and developing into a fully rounded person are all part of this process, as I have described in this chapter.

A heart for tomorrow's church

7

Conclusion

Having read this book, does it seem to you that we have thought of everything and tried to cover all bases to help young people develop into promising building material for the Church of tomorrow? It is true that I discovered that we have done just that as I tried to analyse how our strategy for young people developed over the years. However, without God's help and guidance none of what we have attained would be possible. He loves young people much more than we do. He has been the inspiration and the challenge behind all these ideas and He has faithfully provided us with all the people, finances and materials to make it all possible.

You might wonder if it is all very well going to all that effort for the young people and children in your church but what do you do to reach others? We have found that it is a natural progression. If other young people see plenty of young people in the church who are obviously happy and excited about their God - they want to come to the church too to find out what is different about them. The young people from the church cannot help but stand out as different wherever they are and at some point curiosity overwhelms others and they begin to ask questions. Community and a sense of belonging are most important to young people. What better place than to find their lives totally transformed by the power of Jesus Christ and to belong to His family the church that loves and cares for them!

The three-fold cord

I wrote about the three-fold cord in the last chapter as the basic principle upon which we have relied. It has proven invaluable as a foundation for retaining teenagers for the Church of tomorrow. It has been essential in keeping the children and young people in the church so that their faith remains vibrant into adulthood and they become invaluable members of the local church, and this is certainly one of our passions. This provides children with a firm foundation upon which they are able to withstand the pressures and temptations that come from the world when they go onto their jobs or university.

Children deserve the best we can give them. We want to prepare young people for life, so that they have all the tools in place with which to succeed in any area of secular employment they choose to enter. The implementation for ministry of this passion involves a tremendous investment of time, energy and money on the part of many people. So many of the members of Peniel Church are involved in investing their time, talents and energy into the young people of Peniel Academy and the church on a day to day basis. They know that the young people will be the Church of tomorrow.

We have a responsibility to ensure our children are raised in a Godly environment. If you want to help ensure your children's future is not corrupted by legislation that erodes our core religious beliefs you can become part of the Christian Congress for Traditional Values (CCTV). The CCTV is a Christian pressure group dedicated to upholding traditional family values. Find out how you can make a difference at www.thecctv.org.

God is no respecter of persons. **If He can do it for us, He can do it for you too.** My husband always tells people to start with what they have, however small, and God will provide the way ahead. We started the church with three people in our living room in 1976 and we started the school with 17 children in a converted stable in 1981. God has increased everything at a very steady pace so that we are proud of what He has accomplished over many years. Everything has stood the test of time because the foundation has been built on Jesus Christ as the chief cornerstone (Eph. 2:20).

I repeat what was written earlier - **anything done in the name of Christ should be synonymous with excellence.** Let me encourage you to do something positive and valuable for the sake of your children and the future of the church of Jesus Christ. Jesus said that He has opened a door that no man can shut (Rev. 3:8). The door is open, as far as the law of the land is concerned, to start Christian schools and colleges. Be encouraged to take advantage of the situation before it is too late!

Michael Reid Ministries does occasionally run seminars on how to start a Christian school which includes a visit to our school. We want to help you in whatever way we can. We do not provide financial help because the same God who provided for us will provide for you. However, do write or email us with any questions you may have.

You will find details of how to contact us at the back of this book.

As Christians, we should be the leaders in producing well developed young people in body, mind and spirit. These young people are the future leaders of the Church of tomorrow and will be a blessing to any nation where they choose to reside and work. **There is hope for the next generation!**

The most important thing is to be able to see with your own eyes and experience something that is working in order for your faith rise to the challenge, and to realise that all things are possible with God. I have been inspired by what I have seen throughout the world.

Come and see.

If you would like to read more, you can buy my complete thesis online at: http://www.MichaelReidMinistries.org

Endnotes

[1]Peter Brierley, *The Tide is Running Out,* (London: Christian Research, 2000), 93.

[2]Brierley 129.

[3]George Barna, *Real Teens A Contemporary Snapshot of Youth Culture*, (Ventura, CA: Regal Books, 2001), 136.

[4]Bill Wilson, *Whose Child Is This*, (Florida: Creation House, 1992), 52.

[5]Charles H. Spurgeon, *A Far Reaching Promise*, sermon no 2586, vol. 44 of 63, 1898, The C. H. Spurgeon Collection [CD-ROM] (Albany, OR: AGES Software, 1998), 548.

[6]Spurgeon, *A Far Reaching Promise*, 552.

[7]Gordon J. Wenham, *Word Biblical Commentary Genesis 1-15*, Vol. 1, ed. John D. W. Watts (Waco, TX: Word Books, 1987), 71.

[8]Duane L. Christensen, *Deuteronomy 1-11*, Word Biblical Commentary, vol. 6A, edited by John D.W. Watts (Dallas, TX: Word Books, 1991), 144.

[9]Christensen, 144. (original emphasis).

[10]Charles H. Spurgeon, *Brought Out, To Be Brought In*, Sermon No. 2511, Vol. 44 of 63, 1886, in The C. H. Spurgeon Collection, [CD-ROM] (Albany, OR: AGES Software, 1998).

[11]Charles H. Spurgeon, *The Child Samuel's Prayer*, Sermon No 586, Vol 10 of 63, 1864, in The C. H. Spurgeon Collection, [CD-ROM] (Albany, OR: AGES Software, 1998).

[12]Allen P. Ross, *Proverbs*, The Expositor's Bible Commentary, vol. 5, edited by Frank E. Gaebelein (Grand Rapids, MI: Zondervan, 1991), 982.

[13]D M Lloyd Jones, *Life in the Spirit in Marriage, Home and Work*, (Edinburgh, UK and Carlisle, PE: Banner of Truth Trust, 1998), 279.

[14]Lloyd Jones, *Darkness and Light*, (Edinburgh, UK and Carlisle, PE: Banner of Truth Trust, 1982), 227.

[15]Dr James C. Dobson, *Parenting isn't for Cowards*, (Thomas Nelson Publishing Group, 1987), 19.

[16]Leslie J. Francis and William K. Kay, *Teenage Religion and Values* (Leominster, UK: Gracewing Fowler Wright Books, 1995), 81.

[17]Wesner Fallaw, *The Modern Parent and the Teaching Church*, (New York: MacMillan Co., 1960), 185.

[18]Fallaw, 172.

[19]Mark W. Cannister, "Early Adolescence" in *Evangelical Dictionary of Christian Education*, ed. M J Anthony (Grand Rapids, MI: Baker Academic of Baker Book House, 2001), 222.

[20]Barna, 19.

[21]"Peniel Pentecostal Church Congregational Attitudes and Beliefs Survey 2001" in *Research Report* (London: Christian Research, Nov 2001), 40.

[22]Barna, 149.

[23]William R. Yount, *Created to Learn* (Nashville, TN: Broadman and Holman Publishers, 1996), 185.

[24]Barna, 159.

[25]Oral Roberts, *Expect a Miracle: My Life and Ministry: An Autobiography* (Nashville, TN: Nelson Publishers, 1995), 162.

[26]Daryl Eldridge, *The Teaching Ministry of the Church: Integrating Biblical Truth with Contemporary Application* (Nashville, TN: Broadman and Holman, 1995), ix.

[27]Francis and Kay, 186. (author's parenthesis).

[28]Brierley, *Peniel Pentecostal Church Survey*, 35. (original emphasis).

[29]Martin Luther, "Table Talk," in *Luther's Works*, vol. 54, edited by T.G. Tappert (Philadelphia: Fortress Press, 1967), 235.

[30]Mark Fenn, "Warning for Unruly Pupils - Zero Tolerance Crackdown on Bad Behaviour," *Brentwood Gazette*, 1 September 2004, 1.

[31]Alexandra Freen, "We are not Keen to Fight, but We Do Want the Cane Back," *The Times* (London), 13 September 2004, 6.

[32]Vince Avery, Trumpet Call Newspaper, Issue 34, 28.

[33]"Faith Based Schools Put to the Test," *Idea: Resourcing Members of the Evangelical Alliance to Change Society*, March/April 2002, 20.

[34]Ibid

[35]Roberts, 183.

[36]Marvin R. Wilson, *Our Father Abraham: Jewish Roots of the Christian Faith* (Grand Rapids, MI: Eerdmans Publishing Company, 1989), 303.

[37]Letter from Miss W Sanderson, Independent Schools Registration Team to Rt Rev M S B Reid, Peniel Church, Brentwood, Essex, UK, 19 January 2000.

[38]http://www.timesonline.co.uk/tol/life_and_style/education/a_level_gcse_results/, The Times Online (accessed March 2008).

[39]Susan D. Hill, "Christian Kids at Risk in the Christian School Environment," *Christian Educator's Journal*, Issue 22 (October 2003).

[40]Barbara Lantin, "The Fear of Uncertainty", *Daily Telegraph* (London), 16 September 2004, 22.

MIRACLES·HEALING·FAITH

MICHAEL REID
—MINISTRIES—

Building on the foundation of our biblically based family ethos, and
our focus on miracles, healing and faith, the church expands under
God-anointed leadership. With the Word of God as our touchstone, we
are a voice to the nations through evangelism, education and excellence.

Invitation

You are warmly invited to attend Church services at Michael Reid Minisitries, where healing and miracles happen today. Come and see what God can do for you! Regular meetings: Friday 7.30pm and Sunday 10am.

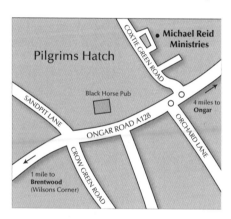

Michael Reid Ministries
49 Coxtie Green Rd
Pilgrims Hatch
Brentwood
Essex
CM14 5PS
ENGLAND

Tel: +44 (0)1277 372996
Fax: +44 (0) 1277 375046

Directions:

M25: Exit 28. Take A1023 to Brentwood. Continue along High St to double roundabout (Wilson's Corner). Turn left, keep going straight for about a mile, then follow map.

A12: Leave at M25 junction, then as above.

A127: Leave at A128 junction. Take A128 to Brentwood. Continue to double roundabout (Wilson's Corner). Turn left, keep going straight for about a mile, then follow map.

A13: Take A128 to Brentwood, then as above.

Church

Founded by Michael and Ruth Reid as a small Bible study group in their home in 1976, Peniel Church has grown to hundreds of members, with connections worldwide.

There are over 40 nationalities represented in the Peniel Church congregation, all united by their faith in Jesus Christ.

Choir

The Peniel Choir started in 1989 with 23 people. Today, it has over 100 choristers and musicians, all of whom are committed Church members.

Members come from all walks of life. Their lives have been transformed by the living God. Their ministry in song challenges and encourages their hearers with the Gospel message.

Television

Michael Reid Ministries unique TV show "What God Can Do For You" was first aired in 2002 and is now broadcast daily into five continents. The shows are packed with miracle testimonies, practical teaching, lively discussion and ministry by the Peniel Choir, and are also streamed worldwide on the internet.

www.MichaelReidMinistries.tv

Publishing

Michael Reid Ministries has always promoted the Gospel through the development of quality Christian material.

Thousands of our magazines, books, DVDs, CDs, MP3s, tapes and videos, which document evidence of the miraculous grace of God can now be found in virtually every nation around the globe.

www.MichaelReidPublishing.com

College

"Study to shew thyself approved unto God, a workman that needeth not to be ashamed, rightly dividing the word of truth." (2 Tim 2:15)

Peniel College offers programmes at Bachelors, Masters and PhD level through affiliations with Oral Roberts University, Tulsa, Oklahoma, and the University of Bangor, Wales.

www.pche.ac.uk

Global Gospel Fellowship

The Global Gospel Fellowship (GGF) was founded in 2000 by Bishop Reid and TL Osborn as an organisation which would encourage fellowship amongst Christian leadership. Today GGF is an interdenominational fellowship that not only enriches people spiritually but provides practical help and resources to church leaders worldwide.

www.tggf.org

School

Peniel Academy was founded in 1982 by Bishop Michael Reid. Starting with a roll of just 17 pupils, the school has now grown to over 150, and its expansion has seen it move to the magnificent 74-acre site at Brizes Park on the outskirts of Brentwood.

The emphasis in the school is on excellence. The children thrive in an environment where the church, the staff and the parents are united. Their focus is to achieve the best for the children in an holistic way - body, mind and spirit.

The cornerstone of the school is its Christian ethos which delivers a clear moral standard and code of behaviour. Pupils are inspired by staff who are a living testimony to honesty, industry and personal integrity.

www.PenielAcademy.ac

Website

Starting in June 1996, the world-class Michael Reid Ministries website contains a wealth of teaching, articles, audio sermons, TV shows, video downloads and products which will challenge and inspire. The internet has provided a unique forum to promote the Gospel directly into people's homes and across the world.

www.MichaelReidMinistries.org

Books

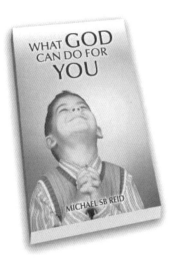

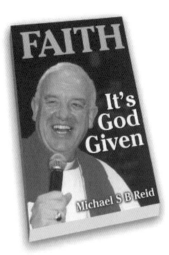

Order: UK: +44(0)1277 372996 USA: 877-487-4722

What God Can Do For You

"Cutting through the veneer of religion, legalism and ritual that so often veils the face of what the Church is meant to be; this book reveals the core values of the Gospel – 'Christ and nothing more, Christ and nothing less, Christ and nothing else'." *JOHN GLASS, Elim Pentecostal Churches UK*

It's So Easy!

A truth so powerful, yet so simple that even a child can understand it.

"The most powerful motivational force in the world is the grace of God. Every Christian needs a revelation of God's grace. This book will open your spiritual eyes... read on." *TERRY LAW, World Compassion Ministries*

"This story of his conversion and subsequent global miracle ministry is unique." *TL OSBORN, Osborn International*

"...A big man with a big personality doing a big work for a big God....This book...will inspire you to reach out to the God who can do much more than you can ask or imagine." *PETER KERRIDGE, Premier Radio, UK*

www.MichaelReidPublishing.com

Faith: It's God Given

   This book, packed with dynamic illustrations and truths of scripture, is written for those who are sick of the false 'faith' emphasis that condemns and discourages, and will realign your thinking to the true Biblical faith in Christ.

   The inspired simplicity of Bishop Reid's message brings a new hope and understanding as he urges his readers to abandon their understanding and accept that GOD ALONE CAN DO IT.

Strategic Level Spiritual Warfare: A Modern Mythology?

   "Don't touch this, it's dangerous!" quipped Michael Reid at a bookfair in the USA.

   If you want to know the truth about spiritual warfare, then this is the book for you.

   It will focus your understanding on the Biblical, historical and theological background to the phenomena of spiritual warfare. Armed with this information, it will enable you to live and walk in Christ's total victory.

Order: UK: +44(0)1277 372996 USA: 877-487-4722

DVDs

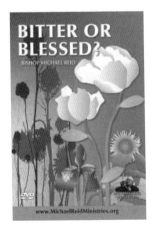

www.MichaelReidPublishing.com

Audio CDs

Have a Grateful Heart

Christ in Me

Oranges & Lemons

What Drives You?

Order: UK: +44(0)1277 372996 USA: 877-487-4722

Make a Difference

Become a partner! Michael Reid Ministries is active around the world, providing life-changing spiritual and material help. It is supported entirely by free-will contributions of our friends and partners. For more information about how you can get involved, please visit our website.

www.MichaelReidMinistries.org/partners/

ABOUT THE AUTHOR

Dr Ruth Reid, wife of Bishop Michael Reid, founder of Michael Reid Ministries, has worked alongside her husband for over 30 years. She has travelled across the globe, speaking at various conventions and women's meetings, taking the truth of the gospel. She also travels ahead of her husband to prepare the way for the various crusades and conferences that he holds worldwide.

Her real passion, particularly in the last 10 years, has been to encourage churches and pastors to develop the Church of tomorrow. Indeed, the subject of her thesis for her Doctor of Ministry was the retention of young people in churches. Ruth is keen to see churches around the world filled with young people, all born again and fulfilling the life of a Christian, taking the gospel into their world.

Her down to earth, practical teaching on the role of women in ministry, how to bring up children, and how to be a good wife as God intends, has impacted lives and families across the globe.

Ruth holds a degree in Sociology and Chinese from Leeds University and a Diploma in Applied Social Studies from Cardiff University, which qualified her to work as a child care officer before moving into full time ministry. She also holds an MA in Practical Theology and a Doctor of Ministry from Oral Roberts University, Tulsa, Oklahoma and an honorary Doctor of Divinity from Benson Idahosa University, Benin, Nigeria.

She and her husband, Bishop Reid, host their own television programme "What God Can Do For You" which reaches people throughout the world with the Gospel.

Ruth lives with her husband in Essex, England, and they have three grown-up children, and five grandchildren.